In or Out of Season

In or Out of Season

poems

Jane Blanchard

Cover art: most of *Three Pots of Tulips,* Claude Monet, 1883
Cover design: Shay Culligan

ISBN: 978-1-952326-09-7

Kelsay Books
502 South 1040 East, A-119
American Fork, Utah 84003

In memory of Marion Wash,

my STAR teacher

at the Academy of Richmond County

and throughout Richmond County in 1980

Acknowledgments

Poems in this collection have first been published as follows:

Adanna: "Knocked Out"

Anglican Theological Review: "Love Came Down"

The Asses of Parnassus: "So Gone"

Avocet: "poolside palmetto . . ."

Belle Rêve: "Bio" – "Chutney"

Blinking Cursor: "tree out with the trash . . ."

Blue Unicorn: "Drift" – "Knell"

Bones III: "Roadkill"

Carbon Culture Review: "Sewanee"

Calvary Cross: "all is vanity . . ." – "Epiphany" – "Noël"

Cat & Dog Tales: "morning commuters . . ."

Dactyl: "Notes"

The Dead Mule School of Southern Literature: "Jaunt"

The Enigmatist: "'Birds can't be in here!'" – "Vespers"

Enter the Gateway: "Pass It On"

ETC: "A Priori" – "Erasure" – "Resolution" – "Syllogism"

haikuniverse: "crepe myrtle in bloom . . ."

Hitherto: "Of Age"

The Ignatian: "Anecdotal"

Joys of the Table: "A Moveable Meal"

Leaves of Ink: "monarch butterflies . . ." – "answering
machine . . ."

Light: "Cell"

Literature Today: "Rumination"

Lucidity Poetry Journal: "Carillon"

The Lyric: "Missive"

Meat for Tea: "New Orleans"

Mediterranean Poetry: "Scenes"

Mezzo Cammin: "Wings and Things" – "Writer's Retreat"

miller's pond: "Consolation" – "Method"

Orbis: "Campaign"

Pay Attention: "Faux Pas"

The Penwood Review: "Advent" – "Creation"

POEM: "Siren"

The Poetry Porch: The Sonnet Scroll: "Wash and Wear"

Poetry Salzburg Review: "At the James Brown Arena" – "Ode"

RiverSedge: "Uncorked"

The Seventh Quarry: "Encounter" – "Slope"

The Shepherd's Voice: "Fraction"

SLANT: "Anywhere, United States of America"

Snakeskin: "Breviary" – "Old Math"

Tar River Poetry: "Marriage in the Middle Ages"

The Tau: "Compline" – "Transactions"

THINK: "Avowed"

Time of Singing: "To Any and All, Regarding Routine"

TRINACRIA: "Confession" – "Contributors" – "Wheeling and
   Dealing"

Turbulence: "Ivy"

Website of the Great River Shakespeare Festival: "Epistle"

Website of the Society of Classical Poets: "Bewintered" – "SOP"

WestWard Quarterly: "Contacts"

Poems in this collection have been reprinted as follows:

Artemis: "Pass It On"

The Font: "Wash and Wear"

Last Call: "Uncorked"

Mediterranean Poetry: "Transactions"

The Orchards Poetry Journal: "Contacts"

The Shepherd's Voice: "Creation" – "Pass It On"

The Society of Classical Poets Journal: "Bewintered"

Stones before the Ocean: "Fraction"

TRINACRIA: "A Priori"

WestWard Quarterly: "Noël"

"Epistle" was a Laureate's Choice winner in the 2015 Maria Faust
Sonnet Contest.

Contents

"While the earth remains,
Seedtime and harvest,
Cold and heat,
Winter and summer,
And day and night
Shall not cease."

Genesis 8:22

Wash and Wear

The man had two pairs of pants—black and tan.
Shirts varied more in color, not in style—
collars were splayed and tieless. The textile
was always some synthetic rather than
cotton or wool. His lessons, though, were real—
the quirks of English grammar; the techniques
of playwrights, poets, novelists; the piques
of essayists; the tropes of all such spiel.
I learned much from the man, despite the fact
I donned the latest fashions as a belle
of arts and letters. Once cast, I played well
the model student—eager and exact.
Decades later, my wardrobe is quite plain;
a love of language is what I retain.

Of Age

When I returned to poetry
Some years ago, belatedly,
I feared my mind was past its prime,
So I wrote fast to make up time.

But now that I am older still,
Speed does not yield the same quick thrill;
Content to keep a slower pace,
I write at ease, let others race.

Confession

I'm kept. So, there—I've said it. I admit
my husband cultivates—and counts—the beans
that feed us both. Sometimes I feel a bit
indulged or spoiled—imprisoned by no means.

I used to earn a living—now I live
unfettered by a job. I used to grade
too many lousy papers—now I sieve
refined poetic language as a trade.

I still clean house—the tasks the maid declines
to do. And shop—and cook, a lot—except
when better half wants to. That man resigns
himself to service—daily he's adept.

If truth be told, he has his work, I mine—
oh, Lord, I just stole part of that last line.

Marriage in the Middle Ages

With supper done, and dishes, too, a clock
says seven-forty-five, so there is time
for television, exercise, but sleep
has more appeal. The wife goes first, puts on
a gown, begins to read. The husband soon
retires as well, undresses, gets in bed.

A magazine awaits him on a bed-
side table, so he picks it up; his clock
says eight-fifteen. He starts to scan, but soon
eyes fail, hands fall, and wife says it is time
to turn his lamp off. Hers, of course, stays on
a little longer while she flirts with sleep.

However, in the dark she finds that sleep
has lost all interest, and the queen-size bed
becomes uncomfortable. Her spouse flips on
his chest; hers is too big for that. Wife's clock,
its button pressed, says ten-something, past time
for snoozing. Husband starts to snore too soon.

Then box fan does its job, and none-too-soon
its ready, steady hum lulls wife to sleep.
Some hours later, husband knows it's time
for bathroom break; he tries to leave the bed
quite quietly, but she awakens; her clock
says two. When he comes back, the night goes on.

They both drift off again; then wife feels on
fire: hot flashes rage like hell, and soon
she tosses covers to cool down. His clock
says four. The moon lights up the room as sleep
reluctantly returns to both in bed
who wonder when to call it quitting time.

Before they do, dreams commandeer the time
till dawn as each exhausted spouse is on
some random train to who knows where. Their bed
becomes a winking, blinking junction. Soon
nods turn to nudges; limbs are flailing. Sleep
jumps the fast track just after six o'clock.

Caffeine consumed in time, the couple soon
go back to bed. (But why, if not for sleep?)
It's on to work before it's eight o'clock.

Knocked Out

Trimming the remnants of roses,
    I wonder when
        these bushes will bloom again.

Is there time for another
    burst of color
        this late in the season?

Must summer yield to autumn
    and autumn to winter
        before spring puts out pink?

Scenes

from Bread Loaf in Sicily

lost in Erice

man and woman arm in arm

slide down cobblestones

as owl hoots hello

beside hotel balcony

clouds eclipse the moon

blue bleeds into blue

sky above with sea below

beyond Erice

Slope

Most often going up is hard
     compared to coming down,
but either inclination can
     induce a smile or frown.

Expression is determined by
     the way a hill is viewed,
perspective that primarily
     depends on attitude.

Transactions

in Sicilia

The merchant was polite as I came in
on Monday afternoon to browse for wine,
but conversation happened only when
we spoke the common language of the vine.

A dozen bottles were selected, then
examined, labels studied, line by line,
at last set back into the proper bin,
except for one most likely to taste fine.

It did, so I returned to that same store
throughout the week and found the bill to be
a little less each time. I said no more
than *grazie,* smiling ever pleasantly.

By Saturday, I had a patron's status,
awarding me a bar of chocolate gratis.

Uncorked

When buying wine,
imported or domestic,
I rarely find reviews,
in print or online,
that serve me well.
I've just never felt an urge
to drink anything
with notes of crushed rock
or undertones of forest floor.
I'd rather not blend licorice
with lavender or lead pencil
at any point of fermentation.
Cherries and berries are okay,
but why add tobacco or espresso
to the bouquet?
I simply don't care if a wine is
sexy or kinky,
opulent or flamboyant;
and I'm certainly not interested
in knowing whether or not
it has good drainage
and a long finish.
Frankly, I'm afraid of a vintage
that's too exuberant,
full-bodied, and penetrating,
especially if it shows some
secondary characteristics from bottle age.
Do the people who write
such rhetoric really expect me
to take them seriously?

If so, they have clearly imbibed
so many fruits of the vine
that their brains have become
vats of verbiage
left on the lees too long.

Fraction

Restored by God to dignity,
let us behold the bread and wine,
as priest invokes the mystery
of grace ordained by love divine.

Then, one by one and pew by pew,
let us approach, partake the host,
sip from the cup, give thanks unto
the Father, Son, and Holy Ghost.

To Any and All, Regarding Routine

Gather ye manna while ye may,
 The sun is fast a-rising;
Collect enough to last the day
 By your best-yet surmising.

Go forth into the dusty field
 To find the hoary flakes;
Then pound whatever is the yield
 And shape your share of cakes.

The baking or the boiling of
 The same will set your table;
Be sure to thank the Lord above
 As well as you are able.

Leave nothing for tomorrow so
 Of worms ye may be free;
The day that lies ahead will show
 You fresh anxiety.

A Moveable Meal

Regardless of the day, the month, the season,
Mouths must be fed, and well, or within reason.

This mother on vacation wants a venue
That offers family favorites on the menu.

The options can be more or less extensive,
As long as no one's choice is too expensive.

One sunny afternoon, I get the notion
To try a place that overlooks the ocean.

So off we go: despite no reservation,
We get seats soon and start a conversation.

Talk falters once the food comes to the table,
But still we chat and chew as each is able.

Then both male teens succumb to such distraction
That they begin to have the same reaction.

Apparently they find it hard to swallow
While staring at the feast their eyes must follow.

The challenge is to focus on paninis
When girls out on the beach are in bikinis.

poolside palmetto

top lopped by summer labor

too few fronds remain

Erasure

When faculties degenerate,
a person may procrastinate
about tests to investigate
what time tends to substantiate.

It is so hard to concentrate
with little left to stimulate,
expenses still to estimate,
executors to designate.

Some choices others might berate
if they mistakenly equate
care with control of an estate
that will continue to abate.

Life could decline to such a state
that death would seem to come too late
since nothing can prevent the fate
of brain returning to blank slate.

Encounter

I met a moth this morning
When getting on an elevator.
I gave it ready warning
About the fate it would face later.

The light inside looked stronger
Than any seen when doors were parted.
Ride done, I stayed no longer,
But turned to wish moth well, then darted.

Syllogism

Since time is ruthless with the truth,
Most efforts to reclaim lost youth
Appear inept, or worse, uncouth.

And such can even be unwise,
If each is just an exercise
In seeking what old age denies.

For special lotions, potions, pills,
Procedures, programs, diets, drills
May lead to but a stack of bills.

What good are those to any heirs?
To juniors, seniors' constant cares
Prove vanity has many snares.

We all must meet death face-to-face.
Why not display uncommon grace
By smiling, lines of life in place?

all is vanity

under the sun or elsewhere

make peace with pleasure

New Orleans

A way to see lots of this city,
Including some sites that are pretty,
Is to hop on a trolley
That goes slowly, by golly,
But faster would be such a pity.

There are several collections of art
Full of pieces that set them apart,
From worlds old and new,
All ready to view;
It is hard to know just where to start.

Not far from the charming French Quarter
Is a park where a person can loiter
And watch every ship
On the great Mississipp
Make its way to or from open water.

A really assiduous waiter
May recommend getting the gator,
With soup full of turtle
In cream yet to curdle,
Plus coffee and chocolate mousse later.

It is common to feel rather queasy,
Sort of greasy, perhaps even sleazy,
When a bit too much booze
Has gone down with the blues
In a joint somewhere in the Big Easy.

Rumination

Since my last party here at home
    Was many moons ago,
Perhaps I should compile a list
    Of all the folks I know.

It could be easy, even fun,
    To be a host again,
As long as I remember to
    Include more friends than kin.

But even friends can eat or drink
    Too much or not enough,
And some of their companions talk
    About insipid stuff.

A few appear to suffer such
    Severe anxiety
That they must keep a phone nearby
    For all to hear or see.

And what about the ones who tend
    To over-scrutinize
And scarcely leave before they start
    To hyper-criticize?

Thus, by the time I think about
    Whom to invite or not,
The urge to entertain at all
    Has lessened quite a lot.

Consolation

I'm sorry she turned you down flat.
You didn't deserve that a bit.
She thinks of you just as a friend?
That is not what you wanted to hear.

She doesn't deserve you a bit.
I've never been prouder of you!
That is not what you wanted to hear?
You'll never find somebody else?

How could I be prouder of you?
You didn't make any mistake.
Of course, you'll find somebody else!
You'll only feel strange for a while.

She certainly made a mistake.
She'll be sorry she turned you down flat.
You're sure to feel strange for a while.
Can you think of her just as a friend?

Campaign

What woman really wants a diamond advertised
as conflict-free and set in eco-friendly gold?
Such placid and platonic cant has been devised
by one without an epic vision, surely old
but newly true. A man worth salt or more can see
that he must fight, perhaps a while, to score a win.
Mere acquiescence is no certain victory,
for it may well prove pyrrhic, and will do him in.
Thus, even if the wife-to-be is ready, some
rival or parent should arise for all their sakes,
so words and swords can clash, thereby keep lovers from
embracing, then much worse enduring, great mistakes.
Prospective husband, longing not to live alone,
ravage the earth, wage war, kill, die, for that rare stone.

At the James Brown Arena

As a son in a tux
    leads a girl in a gown
        through a waltz on a floor
that is more often used
    for a rodeo ride
        or a furniture fair,
I am taken away
    to a time long ago
        in a Viennese park
when a man bowed and asked
    if I wanted to dance,
        and I looked at my friends,
who then looked back at me,
    and I rose, took his arm,
        and allowed him to lead
me around and around
    for as long as the charm
        of the song would go on.

A Priori

A woman who has found a man
    She thinks she wants to wed
Need not arrange a Rorschach test
    To look inside his head.

A study of his closet should
    Provide her quite a show:
If what he wears is who he is,
    What else is there to know?

His neckties in and of themselves
    May oddly prove to be
A means of learning lots about
    His personality.

Perhaps, more than a few were gifts,
    But some he bought himself.
So, how are they arranged? In bins?
    Hung up? Thrown on a shelf?

As far as colors go, how bold
    Or subtle are the hues?
Warm reds, cool blues, or neutrals can
    Provide important clues.

Regarding images? Dogs? Frogs?
    Insignia? Which types?
And patterns? None? Medallions? Neats?
    Plaid, paisley, grids, or stripes?

Materials? Wool? Cotton? Silk?
    How long? How wide? How old?
Condition? Stained or frayed or clean?
    Unworn, if truth be told?

Additional perspectives could
    Be had from other stuff;
An inventory of the ties
    Most often yields enough.

Method

There's more to a fire than a flame,
Or so my dear husband does claim:
Past stacking, there's stoking,
Appropriate poking,
Unless a mere spark is the aim.

Chutney

From within a dated version
of the classic *Joy of Cooking*
falls a recipe that calls for
cranberries and raisins, apple,
onion, celery, as well as
spices and white sugar, in the
fine but faded script of someone
once familiar through a marriage.

After thinking, going shopping,
I start heating, chopping, stirring,
later canning, cooling, cleaning,
until ending up with eight sealed
pint-sized jars, just right for sharing
with old friends and new relations.

Advent

I cut way back on Christmas long ago—
one gift per person, fewer parties, less
church, simpler foods and decorations, no
cards—nothing that caused me or mine much stress.

My goal was—is—to keep fuss minimal,
reduce the usual anxiety,
attend to what—or whom—mere rhymers call
the season's reason—all for family.

Yet late this year I am a bit befuddled—
my newly pregnant daughter—lo!—decided
not to buy, make, bring, take, send—why be muddled
by such?—for baby's sake, so she confided.

Repeatedly, a mystery I sing—
how could a tiny child change everything?

Contacts

Oh, 'tis the season to cull cards
    That fill my Rolodex,
For I had rather not incur
    A new year's jinx or hex.

So let me toss the cards of those
    Who died or moved away,
Went bonkers, bankrupt, off to jail,
    Lost on election day.

Regarding who did what to whom
    At home or club or church,
I should distinguish those that left
    From those left in the lurch.

As for my former colleagues, few
    Have time to stay in touch;
Most are too busy working hard,
    Or not, to ring me much.

Without a doubt I can remove
    The cards of folks who call
Too frequently or late at night
    Or simply not at all.

Love Came Down

My husband handed me a special gift
at dawn: a set of twelve glass ornaments.
I soon began to hang each on the tree:
the partridge, other birds, then rings, birds yet
again, a maid, a lady, and a lord,
a piper, last a drummer. Hook by hook
held fast to supple pine, except for that
suspending rings. The heart-shaped piece fell to
the hardwood floor and shattered. Startled, I
could not stop tears from forming, overflowing.
Before I could go fetch a broom to sweep
away the mess, I heard my husband say:
"Darling, tell me, what are you crying for?
So one is gone—there are eleven more."

Ode

The package comes well-wrapped—
    Contents intact:

A set of glasses—swell—
    Four by Riedel.

Each rests upon a bowl—
    No stem to hold:

Designed for some gift-list—
    So much is missed.

tree out with the trash

needles swept from floor to door

season's greetings gone

Epistle

Dear Mr. JoS. A. Bank, Esquire, I
am writing to complain about the way
my son and I were treated yesterday
when we had special merchandise to buy.

In short, accessories were needed for
a new tuxedo—so, a shirt with studs,
a bowtie, and a cummerbund: mere duds
were what we found inside your double door.

A manager did greet us, but he sent
the latest hire to make the sale, or not;
the fellow measured sizes, then forgot
that finding them should be his next intent.

Both seemed to want us gone, yet all was fine,
since we went home and ordered—done!—online.

Old Math

Addition is the rule of youth
As life brings skills and jobs and more,
But at some point subtraction starts
To take what did accrue before.

Retirement can deplete too soon
Hard-earned, long-held financial gains,
If all that multiplies with age
Are costs and losses, aches and pains.

Resolution

Perhaps it's time to find a good masseuse.
A chiropractor only helps so much
With all the ails that many years produce.

And exercise makes every ache profuse
And causes me to swallow pills and such;
I lose the time to find a good masseuse.

I'd like to try another lame excuse
To lean on alcohol, a chronic crutch.
(Wines, ales, or booze can any age seduce.)

Again in bed, with pain I call a truce;
A bottle of hot water in my clutch,
I pass the time without a good masseuse.

Though death could bring an end to this abuse,
I'd rather seek relief with lighter touch
And wait for ails the grave will introduce.

Plus, parts of me may still be of some use
Despite confinement in a battered hutch,
So now's the time to find a good masseuse
Who could treat all that ails me like the deuce.

Avowed

You know I'll take good care of you,
whatever happens now or later.
For better, worse, my word is true,
you know. I'll take good care of you—
wealth, health, or not—and do what's due,
to show my love could be no greater.
You know I'll take good care of you,
whatever happens, now or later.

Bewintered

When snow arrives
As long forecast,
It sets a scene
That does not last;

But for the while
Snow sits around,
All else remains
Transfixed, spellbound.

Wings and Things

While it is true—birds of a feather
most often tend to flock together—
my avian menagerie
proves yet the practicality
of tolerating lots that feed
upon the blended stash of seed
available in my back yard
when winter makes survival hard.

Each cardinal with orange bill
must share the trough to eat its fill
with speckled doves which keep good pace
but take up so much perching space
that chickadees, though wee, must then
stand far too close to some stray wren
until a single surly jay
alights and frightens all away.

"Birds can't be in here!"

So says a small girl,
gawking, holding hands
with smaller brother,
standing with Daddy
inside Home Depot.

My husband mutters,
"She's got lots to learn."

Birds have their own rules,
for flying, roosting,
dropping whatever,
whenever nature
calls and doors open.

morning commuters

swerve to miss escapees from

some electric fence

Roadkill

The most recent carnage
on Walton Way
happens to be a red fox,

which is dodged by vehicles
(following the fatal one)
before it is moved

to the far side of the walk,
where it is left
to become a blackened pelt

incapable of sending
even a whiff of stench
from among the pine needles.

Pass It On

As legend goes, the dogwood tree
was cut for use at Calvary.

And ever since that crucial date
it tries to grow more bent than straight.

Its flower, though, of petals four
looks like the cross it forms no more.

Each one is notched, and tinted, too,
as if wounds left both hole and hue.

But each one does its best to hold
a crown of what surpasses gold.

For seeds soon fall upon the ground
and spread the legend all around.

Ivy

Ivy of
the English
variety grows
so quickly that it
soon sneaks out of its
bed and creeps across the
yard and climbs trees to annoy
squirrels and crawls through fences
and over walls to bother all the neighbors.

Notes

once the soldiers go

only the thistle is left

to guard the castle

      [Stirling, 14 June 2013]

all collies must wait

until the shepherd whistles

welcome to the fold

      [Scottish Highlands, 16 June 2013]

sidewalk serenade

proves whisky has no manners

in the wee hours

      [Edinburgh, 18 June 2013]

Anywhere, United States of America

Two stations open, the long line gets longer,
as busy customers arrive to glower
at each unhurried, harried postal monger.

A man wants mail without ID; though wrong or
worse, still he argues for a quarter hour:
two stations open, the long line gets longer.

The woman with a toddler tag-alonger
just must insure each package in the tower
she hurls at one much-harried postal monger.

A lady—next—needs stamps; despite the throng, her
vast voice demands more choice than flag or flower:
two stations open, the long line gets longer.

The guy behind is not a great prolonger;
a debit reading—zero—makes him cower,
then hurry from a gray-haired postal monger.

An urge arises and grows stronger,
to be a UPS/FedEx avower:
two stations open, the long line gets longer,
no hurry from a harried postal monger.

SOP

(Standard Operating Procedure)

I never answer any call
    That shows ID unknown;
Anonymous cannot persuade
    Myself to get the phone.

Thus, any private number/name
    Must speak to my machine;
When I see data incomplete,
    I always choose to screen.

So Gone

There once was a comet named ISON,
A grazer who gave gazers such fun;
Then it went way too close
To the sun—adios!
Astronomers' work was much undone.

Creation

Once God made light, He bid it stay
Apart from dark, and all was good
On earth that first and special day.

Then came the dome, a fine display
Dividing zones, as well it could
Once God made sky and bid it stay.

Next waters parted and gave way
To land so trees, plants, grasses would
Fill all the earth from that third day.

Then came sun, moon, stars, an array
Of seasons, not yet understood
By birds and fishes made to stay.

Next animals appeared so they
Might welcome Adam, Eve, who should
Have lived in peace on earth each day.

With works complete, none yet astray,
God paused, foresaw a likelihood,
And last made rest, then bid it stay
For all on earth each seventh day.

Noël

Welcome, small one, grandchild of mine!
May all you are and do on earth
Remind you of the great design
That brought about your day of birth.

May you grow strong and wise and fine;
May work and play and rest give mirth;
May sun and moon upon you shine;
May you trust God for faith and worth.

Missive

It looks to be a typed appeal
Prepared with some religious zeal.

Before I find specifics out,
I guess what it might be about.

Do people with no cash to spare
Need medical or dental care?

Has recent storm or quake or spill
Left work for all with any skill?

Do children lack a special school
In which to learn the golden rule?

Is gospel to be shared through song
To every soul who comes along?

Whatever and wherever, though,
The writer really wants to go.

Thus, he or she is asking me
To show my faith through charity.

The hope is that God's will be done,
But, gosh, this venture might prove fun.

And I could help if I would pray
Or, better, send a check today.

Faux Pas

There are some things
One should not say
To someone else
By night or day.

Are you alone?
That so? No date?
Looks like we may
Have met by fate.

I see you wear
No wedding band.
How would you like
A one-night stand?

What do you do?
Executive?
What firm? Indeed?
Well, gotta live.

How long have you
Been out of work?
Are you a dud
Or just a jerk?

Which Ivy is
Your alma mater?
You went to State?
Must be a plodder.

This week I ran
A marathon.
Can you bend down
To put shoes on?

It's been a while
Since last we met.
Why haven't you
Tried Botox yet?

Divorced again?
How do you cope?
With therapy
Or prayer or dope?

And so you found
A church that fits?
Too bad it's full
Of hypocrites.

Republican
Or Democrat?
Not registered?
And why is that?

Which son of yours
Might go to jail?
The trial is when?
How much was bail?

Your daughter—did
She finish school?
And you still pay?
Are you a fool?

How long since you
Spoke to your mother?
Why, shame on you!
You have no other.

By damn, you have
Some daddy issues.
Why bawl at me?
Go look for tissues.

I love your purse!
So, fake or real?
What store or street?
Was it a steal?

Let's have a drink!
Sure, on my tab.
Booze, wine, or beer?
How was rehab?

Such small talk is
Just not polite
For anyone
By day or night.

Wheeling and Dealing

Some peddlers call themselves consultants now:
For sale is what to do and when and how.

A fee or cut gets them to strategize
On matters no one else can quite devise.

They always claim to have the very tool
Befitting government, firm, church, or school.

And should a problem happen with the same,
They can be paid some more to take the blame.

A common cost of all this expertise
Is palms involved begin to feel like grease.

Epiphany

Back in the day I did believe
Lord Jesus once took sin away,
But now I know I was naive
    Back in the day.

For still I err, to my dismay,
And Christ must grant me new reprieve
Each time I yield to Satan's sway.

Not on this earth will I achieve
A life that does not go astray,
A concept I could not conceive
    Back in the day.

Anecdotal

I hitched my wagon to a star
Yet did not travel very far:
A wheel fell off and I was stuck
To make my own way through the muck.

*

I held onto a coattail once
That lacked sufficient tolerance:
The fabric stretched until it tore
And left a scrap but nothing more.

*

I often tried to swim upstream
While in pursuit of some new dream:
The current ever proved so strong
That I gave up before too long.

*

I fell again from that old horse
But hopped back on in all due course:
Each time I sought a better ride
On which I could remain astride.

*

I used to push the envelope
Beyond the point of any hope:
I always got a paper cut
That bled until the wound would shut.

Drift

You find it easy just to drift
through days or weeks or months or years
without a plan while peers
work hard to sift
all options for careers
despite their fears.
You take for granted the great gift
of time as patience cheers
and prudence jeers
your putting off all moves to shift
your life through higher gears.
But destination nears,
and you may need more than short shrift
when fate pulls out her shears
and snips and sneers,
if you get my drift.

monarch butterflies

flitting through the autumn air

near the King and Prince

Vespers

When I begin to yawn and nod,
I emulate Scheherazade
And leave myself a topic to
Develop when the night is through;

Not that I fear to lose my head
Before or after time in bed,
But I do hate to face the day
Without a project underway.

Writer's Retreat

Rising early, donning ready sneakers,
down four sets of stairs she steps to reach the
parking lot, another to the beach, a
route accommodating ocean seekers.

After breakfast, plus a quarter-liter-
cola, she relaxes for an hour
on the Web, then minutes in the shower,
draining condo's meager water heater.

Housework goes so quickly that it borders
on compulsion, but the television's
interruptions do delay decisions:
when and where and what for take-out orders.

All poetic efforts yield such bad rhyme
that she wonders whether just to head home
(without finishing a must-be-read tome)
or to settle for advancing bedtime.

Inspiration can be quite elusive
when a writer tries to be reclusive.

Compline

Too often once I have reclined,
A phrase or clause pops in my mind
For work that I intend to write
As soon as dark gives way to light;

And so I turn to grab a pen
With which to put words there and then
On paper meant to bear my scrawl
And keep me from forgetting all.

answering machine

still taking calls for someone

stuck on island time

Sewanee

I bought a sound machine on Amazon
and packed it for a trip to Tennessee
since sleep can be a rare phenomenon
when staying in a dorm for fee or free.

I knew the setting "ocean waves" would not
work well upon the Cumberland Plateau,
but only when I reached the parking lot
did "waterfall" seem less than apropos.

Real "rain" was what was falling then and there,
four floors below my room in Saint Luke's Hall,
where open windows let in some fresh air
and none blew through a metal vent at all.

Each "summer night" a band of frogs outside
kept me from turning on a "running stream"
or hearing my own "heartbeat" as I tried
to rest before "songbirds" began a theme.

Cell

at Sewanee

Often, within this edifice of stone,
I lose the blasted signal on my phone.

Right in the middle of a rave or rant,
The other voice ("You there?") gets oddly scant.

Depending on the time and day and case,
I may leave here to find a better space;

Or I may stay, decline to call again,
Reserve my battery, and spare my kin.

I have discovered what may seem absurd:
It is enough to talk and not be heard.

Breviary

Ten days into
A writers' conference,
I think that monks
Did right by silence.

Carillon

The bells are fine at first,
Their music not the worst.

Such melodies they peal,
Each rung with striking zeal.

A little after oon,
Starts up the umpteenth tune.

When light begins to drop,
I beg the bells to stop.

crepe myrtle in bloom

from the mountains to the coast

just pink to past peak

Siren

My mate should strap me to the mast
    And let me hear, not heed,
The next call for a conference,
    No matter how I plead.

It is so tempting to head toward
    An opportunity
That offers respite from a life
    At sea with poetry.

But danger lurks when such a song
    Is cast with much allure;
It is far safer just to stay
    Beyond the shore, for sure.

Jaunt

Aboard the ferry in mid-February
the wind-chilled temperature is oddly raw
for writers toting what is necessary
to while away five days on Ossabaw.

Few other creatures note the boat's arrival:
some waterfowl, a feral pig or two.
Most wildlife tends to focus on survival
and tries to overlook what humans do.

Inside the wooden clubhouse meals are served
and meetings held; crude bunks do not prevent
sufficient sleep. Those writers not unnerved
by commentary seem at least content.

Departure runs on time. All feel the loss
of leaving Muses draped in Spanish moss.

Knell

Some editors do not consider rhyme.
Though ballad meter has a tale to tell,
Such work will be rejected every time.

Heroic couplets go unsold a dime
A dozen in this free-for-all-verse spell.
Some editors do not consider rhyme.

Blank verse may be accepted, if sublime.
A triolet or rondeau? Sent to hell.
Such work will be rejected every time.

The sonnet, any style, is past its prime;
That olden form no longer fares so well.
Some editors do not consider rhyme.

Sound overwrought is even thought a crime
Within a roundel or a villanelle.
Such work will be rejected every time.

So, what to do? Just shun the fun of chime;
Let language run around the page pell-mell.
Some editors do not consider rhyme;
Such work will be rejected every time.

Contributors

The list is varied more than usual,
In prose that follows all the poetry;
American or international,
Each writer offers an identity.

Two are professors, one an editor;
Another has laid brick and tended bar;
A former addict is a counselor
Who aims to be a literary star.

One claims to be an Army veteran;
Another is an expert in the law;
A laborer is actually a nun;
A freelancer keeps house in Arkansas.

One raises vegetables, another beef,
A mother her assorted procreation;
A recent graduate is very brief:
She has a single Pushcart nomination.

One has been homeless, still is out of work,
Has published some, but no collection yet;
The library where he is prone to lurk
Provides him access to the Internet.

This issue shows it makes a lot of sense
To limit such to name and residence.

Bio

I've never gone to Disney World,
    Nor have I wanted to;
I'd rather visit some resort
    That caters to the few.

And I am not a Facebook friend
    Of those who do post there;
Instead I write or call the ones
    Who genuinely care.

I power off the Super Bowl
    Soon after it's begun;
Except for ads, the game is not
    What I consider fun.

And Real Housewives or Jersey Shore
    May have devoted fans;
I am not one, and so it goes
    For the Kardashians.

I seldom fill out feedback once
    I purchase stuff online;
I like to save the time it takes
    To write "just fine" or whine.

And I refuse to "comment" on
    An item in the news;
I much prefer my rant or rave
    Get fewer public views.

In any conversation I
    Stay very true to type;
I shun each subject that becomes
    Objectified by hype.

It's strange that I am willing still
    To wait upon the Muse;
Someday, perhaps, I'll recognize
    I've fallen for her ruse.

About the Author

Jane Blanchard divides her time between Augusta and Saint Simon's Island, Georgia. She has three previous collections—*After Before* (2019), *Tides & Currents* (2017), and *Unloosed* (2016)—all with Kelsay Books.

www.ingramcontent.com/pod-product-compliance
Lightning Source LLC
Chambersburg PA
CBHW022014080426
42733CB00007B/600